M.Smart

SUCCESS WITH
SIGHT WORDS

Multisensory Ways to Teach High-Frequency Words

Written by Sara Throop, Ph.D.

Editor: Wendy L. Blocher

Illustrator: Jane Yamada

Designer: Moonhee Pak

Project Director: Carolea Williams

TABLE OF CONTENTS

 KINESTHETIC Activities

 VISUAL Activities

AUDITORY Activities

INTRODUCTION

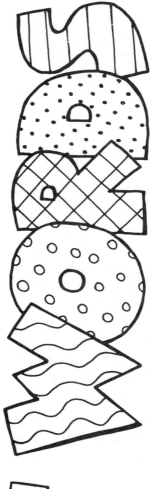

Have you ever been faced with the dilemma of a student who can't recognize *were* from *there?* Do your students find traditional flash-card drills boring and ineffective? Have you been searching for motivating ways to successfully teach those high-frequency or sight words, such as *because, were,* or *said? Success with Sight Words* is a resource that includes a wide selection of hands-on and engaging activities using the kinesthetic, visual, and auditory learning styles to make learning any sight word fun.

There comes a time when reading and writing these essential words, also referred to as high-frequency or sight words, can become challenging for children. Children need strategies to help them read and write these essential words. Ensuring that students learn these words requires more than just having them look at flash cards. Students need to explore and experiment with strategies that help them master and apply these difficult words. At the same time, students need greater opportunities to use reading and writing strategies independently. The multisensory approach in this resource allows students to experience words through taste, touch, smell, sound, and movement.

Success with Sight Words provides teachers with effective, motivating ways to teach high-frequency or sight words. In each activity, children see, hear and use the word in written language to make the learning more meaningful and personal. Included in this resource are a variety of practical, fun, and simple-to-use activities to reinforce these target words. This handy book is filled with games, chants, art projects, and "mouth-watering" activities that make learning any word fun. Integrate the word-wall, management, and parent-involvement ideas into your own reading and writing program.

GETTING STARTED

What Are Sight Words?

Sight words, also referred to as high-frequency words, are typically words students encounter frequently in reading and writing. What makes these words more difficult for students to master is that they do not follow the typical phonetic rules students use in their daily reading and writing. While students are learning words daily, sight words can be more difficult for them to retain since they do not always follow letter-sound relationships. Sight words do not represent easy spelling patterns, but they do appear so frequently in all kinds of text that students become familiar with them but may not necessarily retain or apply them in their own reading and writing. The word list on page 56 includes words that appear most frequently in reading and writing. In order for students to retain a difficult word, they need many opportunities to experience and manipulate it.

Planning

Keep in mind that the activities in this book are generic enough to use with any word. When planning activities, decide which sight words you wish to target. These words can be selected from the Sight Words List/Reading Inventory reproducible (page 56) or they can be any word that presents a problem to a learner.

Use the Weekly Planner reproducible (page 57) to help you plan and organize your activities. Each week photocopy this sheet and keep it in your lesson plan book. Choose new words each week, and write the activity you will do for each day. Activities can be taught as lessons that target a specific sight word or as mini-lessons for a number of words. Many of the activities can be done with a small group, the whole class, or at an independent-learning center. After an activity is done with the whole class, place it in a learning center so students can practice the strategy with different sight words. Invite students to explore and complete the activity on their own in the learning center.

Creating a Sight-Word Classroom Environment

A print-rich classroom environment makes word learning more interesting and fun for students. Create an area in your room completely dedicated to sight words. Begin by making a word wall (see Using a Word Wall, page 8) and displaying it in a large area of the classroom. Remind your students to refer to the word wall when faced with words that present a problem. Use the word wall to complement the activities in this resource, as well as to provide reference support for students in their reading and writing. If you do not have a word wall or plan to implement one into your classroom, write the words on large sheets of construction paper and display them in your classroom. You can also write each letter of the alphabet on a library pocket and display the pockets on a bulletin board. Write sight words on index cards, and place them in the pockets. Students can choose the cards they need and return them to the pockets when they are finished.

Place in a learning center manipulative materials, books, and other resource materials that complement your sight-word learning center. Some suggestions include

- magnetic boards and letters
- pipe cleaners, dough, and other materials that can be used to form letters or words
- letter and word cards
- rubber letter stamps and ink pads
- letter tiles, unifix cubes, beans, pasta, and other materials that can be used to build letters or words
- sentence strips and writing paper
- markers, crayons, and pencils

Introduce the activities to your students as a whole group. Set up activities in the center that students can explore independently or in a small group. It may be necessary for you to work briefly with the small group, depending on the ability of your students. Reteach any lessons or skills you feel are necessary to meet the needs of your class or individual students. Display any completed work from the activities to create a functional word reference center.

Learning Styles

The activities in this book are divided into three sections: kinesthetic, visual, and auditory. Although the ideas and strategies in each section overlap, you can use the Learning Styles Inventory reproducible (page 58) to help you assess each student's learning style and then select the most effective activities. Photocopy this sheet for each student. Complete the inventory based on your observations, and place it in the student's portfolio. You may notice that some students fit easily into one category, while others exhibit two learning styles (e.g., visual-kinesthetic learners). Use the Class Learning Styles reproducible (page 59) to keep a record of your students' learning styles. This will help you group them by their learning styles when planning small-group lessons. Even though some of your students may function best in one modality, it is important to have your students experience all the learning modalities.

Word Bank

A student dictionary or word bank is a very useful tool when students are learning and applying any new word. Invite your students to make their own word bank by having them fold a large sheet of tagboard in half or use folders with paper fasteners inside. Photocopy the Word Bank reproducible (page 60), and give each student 26 copies of it, one for each letter of the alphabet. Have students write a capital and lowercase letter in the square of each page. Photocopy the How about a Try reproducible (page 61) enough times so you can place several copies with each student's word bank. Secure the sheets inside each folder to make a book. Each time you introduce a new sight word, invite students to record it in their word bank on the appropriate alphabet page. Students can also include other troublesome words they encounter in their reading and writing. Invite students to practice writing words from their word bank on the How about a Try reproducible. Students can practice writing the sight words on that page before they interact with the words in the lesson, and they can also write them on this page after the lesson is complete to reinforce letter formation and visual memorization.

Record-Keeping Tips

Evaluation and assessment of each student's progress should be ongoing. Assess growth by observing each student and keeping anecdotal records about his or her participation in the activities. Use the following methods to help you monitor your students' progress:

STUDENT PORTFOLIOS

Invite each student to make a portfolio out of a file folder and decorate it. Store inventories, anecdotal records, writing samples, artwork, and other projects inside the portfolios. If you wish, take pictures of students working on various projects. You can place photos in each student's portfolio or use them as part of a bulletin board display or class book. Share portfolios with students and parents to give them an idea of student progress.

SIGHT WORDS LIST/READING INVENTORY

Use this word list (page 56) to help you assess which words your students need to review. Keep a list in each student's portfolio. Complete a Sight Words Record Sheet reproducible (page 62) for each student to monitor which words he or she has been introduced to, reviewed, or mastered.

GUIDED READING

Listen to the students' oral reading to check for fluency. When a student hesitates, skips a word, or asks for help, note the word with which the student struggled. Print the word on a sticky note or index card, and store it in the student's portfolio. Write the word on the Individual Word Profile reproducible (page 63) to help you plan and organize lessons to meet the needs of that student.

EVALUATION OF WRITTEN WORK

Evaluating student writing provides an opportunity for ongoing assessment. Review each student's written work, and check if any sight words are misused or misspelled on a regular basis. Record your observations on the Writing Assessment reproducible (page 64). For example, look at the student's written work, and write any misused or misspelled words in the first column. Invite the student to write the correct spelling in the next column. In the last column, have students write what they need to remember to help them spell that word correctly. If the same words occur in the child's next piece, note these words again as needing review.

USING A WORD WALL

Students interact with letters and words on a daily basis in the classroom. A classroom environment rich with print is very effective for any student learning to read and write. Word walls provide an opportunity for students to interact with letters and words on a regular basis. A word wall is an organized collection of words written in large print and displayed in an area of the classroom where it can be easily seen. It is not just for display; it is a tool students can use when reading and writing. Designed to promote group learning, a word wall serves as a great classroom tool for individual students.

Many activities in this resource refer to a word wall, which can often be used as a quick and simple tool for many of the lessons. However, if you do not have a word wall or you do not plan to implement one in your classroom at this time, you can write the words on chart paper or the chalkboard or make word cards as an alternative.

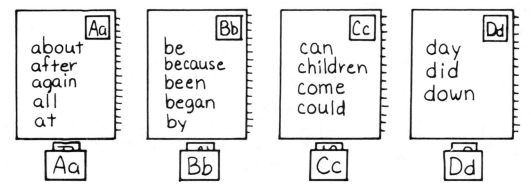

Choosing Words for Your Word Wall

Use the Sight Words List/Reading Inventory reproducible (page 56) to help you choose words for your word wall. Consider starting with the easier words and progressing to the harder ones. Choose words that you wish to introduce to your whole class, as well as words that pose a problem to individual students. All students can benefit from any word on the word wall. Introduce no more than five words per week to be sure students are not overwhelmed.

Making Your Word Wall

Here are some guidelines for making a word wall:

• Make the organization of the word wall visually apparent. For example, words are typically organized in alphabetical order.

• Write the words in large, clear print. Words written on large cards work best. Each time you write a word on a card, invite students to help you decide where the word should be placed on the word wall.

• Label 26 library pockets with each letter of the alphabet and place them in alphabetical order along the bottom of your word wall. Place in each pocket word cards of the sight words. Students can choose the words they need and return them to the pockets when they are finished.

Introducing Words from the Word Wall

Use the word wall as a simple resource for the activities presented in this book. Here are some suggestions for you to keep in mind before adding a new word to the wall:

- Engage your students in a discussion about the structure of the word. For example, you might ask, *How many letters are in the word?*, *What are the beginning letters of the word?*, or *What other words are similar to this word?*

- Write the word on the chalkboard. Invite students to chant the spelling of the word. For variety, students can clap, snap, tap, or use other movements while chanting the spelling of the word.

- Invite students to use their "invisible pencil" to spell the word. Have them write the word with their index finger in the air; on their cheek, leg or arm; or on the floor. Have students write the word three times using their invisible pencil, underlining the word each time.

- Invite students to write words being added to the word wall in their word bank. Encourage students to practice writing the words on the How about a Try page of their word bank.

HOME—SCHOOL CONNECTION

Parents play a key role in the development of their child's learning. Encourage parents to be actively involved by helping in the classroom, donating supplies, and working with their child on nightly homework. Send home the parent letter (page 11) to provide background information on your sight-words study and share some of the activities children will be doing.

Each week send home a Sight Word Contract sheet (page 12) with each student. This sheet suggests activities for parents and children to do together. Many of these activities use items commonly found around the house. To begin, fill in the number of points you expect students to complete for the week. Duplicate the sheet, and send it home the first day of the week. Ask students and parents to return it signed and completed on the last day of the week.

At the end of each week, take time in the classroom for students to discuss the activities they did for the week. The students can take the opportunity to reflect on which activities they liked best. Display any outstanding work your students have completed after they turn in their contract. Place the contracts in the students' portfolios to share with parents at conference time.

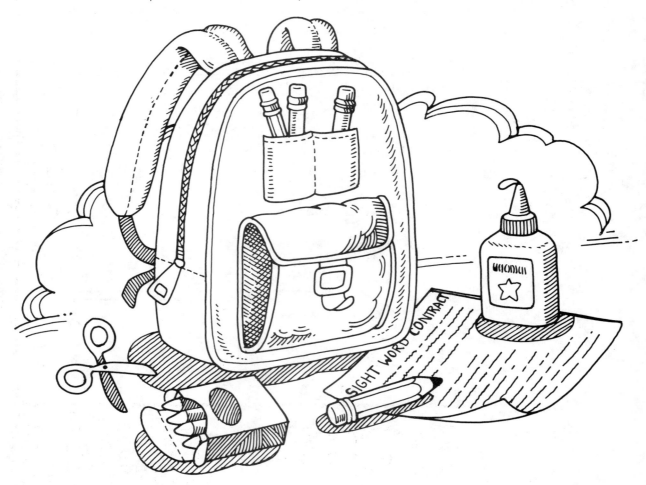

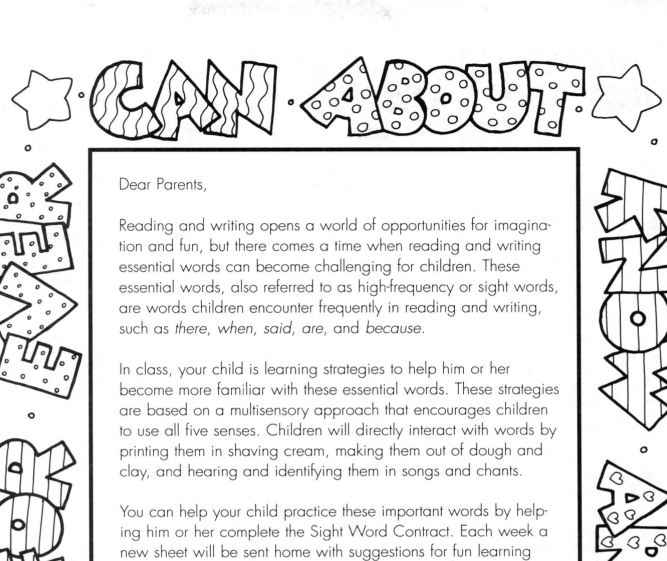

Dear Parents,

Reading and writing opens a world of opportunities for imagination and fun, but there comes a time when reading and writing essential words can become challenging for children. These essential words, also referred to as high-frequency or sight words, are words children encounter frequently in reading and writing, such as *there*, *when*, *said*, *are*, and *because*.

In class, your child is learning strategies to help him or her become more familiar with these essential words. These strategies are based on a multisensory approach that encourages children to use all five senses. Children will directly interact with words by printing them in shaving cream, making them out of dough and clay, and hearing and identifying them in songs and chants.

You can help your child practice these important words by helping him or her complete the Sight Word Contract. Each week a new sheet will be sent home with suggestions for fun learning activities you and your child can complete together. You will not only enjoy your time together, but you will help your child become a more successful reader and writer of sight words.

You and your child will enjoy these special homework times together. These activities will help your child become an enthusiastic and successful reader and writer. Happy word learning!

Sincerely,

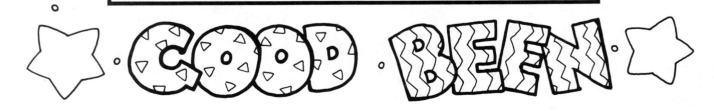

Success with Sight Words © 1999 Creative Teaching Press

SIGHT WORD CONTRACT

Twenty-five Ways to Practice Your Sight Words

For the week of_____ I will complete _____ points.
I will turn in my work at the end of the week with my contract.

Student signature   Parent signature

_____   _____

Words for the Week

_____, _____, _____, _____, _____

Check off each activity you do.

1. Use yarn or string to form your words. (5 pts.)
2. Read a story. See how many times you can find your words. (5 pts.)
3. Print your words with your fingers five or more times in flour, salt, or sugar. (5 pts.)
4. See how many times you can write your words in one minute. (5 pts.)
5. Write three or more sentences using each word. (5 pts.)
6. Use coins to form your words. (5 pts.)
7. Use your favorite snack to shape your words and then eat them. (5 pts.)
8. Tape-record yourself saying and spelling your words. (5 pts.)
9. Print the words on someone's back using your fingers. Have the person guess your words. (5 pts.)
10. Form your words out of small objects such as coins or buttons. (5 pts.)
11. Use colored chalk to write your words on the sidewalk. (5 pts.)
12. Spread peanut butter on bread. Add raisins to form your words. (5 pts.)
13. Use cooked spaghetti to form your words. (5 pts.)
14. Stamp your words using assorted stamps and colors. (5 pts.)
15. Form your words out of alphabet cereal. (5 pts.)
16. Use colored crayons or markers to copy your words in as many different color combinations as possible. (10 pts.)
17. Draw your favorite character saying your words. (10 pts.)
18. Paint your words using watercolors or fingerpaint. (10 pts.)
19. Find the letters of your words in a newspaper. Cut out the letters and spell your words. (10 pts.)
20. Use bread or cookie dough to shape your words and bake them. (10 pts.)
21. Use beans, pasta, or rice to form your words. Glue them to construction paper or tagboard. (10 pts.)
22. Read a letter from the mail. Look for your words and list them. (10 pts.)
23. Write three or more words that rhyme with each of your words. (10 pts.)
24. Fold a sheet of paper in fourths. Write your words one time in each square and decorate the squares with art supplies. (10 pts.)
25. Write a message to someone using your words. (10 pts.)

My favorite activity was _____

because_____.

TEXTURED WORD QUILT

materials

Quilt Square reproducible (page 65)

index cards

glue

assorted colors of torn-paper scraps

crayons or markers

scissors

word bank

butcher paper

In advance, make a photocopy of the Quilt Square reproducible for each student. Write several sight words on separate index cards. Distribute a word card to each student. Have students use their index finger to write their word three times in the air, underlining the word each time. Distribute to each student a quilt square, glue, and assorted colors of torn-paper scraps. Invite students to print their word with a pencil in the center of their quilt square. Have students place a small amount of glue on their fingers and trace over the letters. Ask them to place the paper scraps on the glue and then finish decorating their quilt square with more paper scraps, crayons, or markers. Have students cut out their quilt square and trace their word with their fingers. Ask students to practice writing their word in their word bank for letter formation and memorization. Glue the squares side-by-side on butcher paper. Display the "quilt" on a bulletin board display titled *Stitching Together Sight Words*. Invite students to touch the quilt squares to learn different sight words. Students can use the quilt as a reading and writing resource for future activities.

OUT OF SIGHT

materials

large sheets of
construction paper

glue

dried beans,
pasta, or rice

scissors

word bank

Choose four sight words that start with the same letter, such as *what, when, where,* and *which.* Write the words on the chalkboard. Working with a small group of students, have them clap and chant the words several times. Distribute a large sheet of construction paper to each student. Have students fold their paper into fourths and write one of the words in each quarter. Invite students to trace the words with glue and lay an assortment of dried beans, pasta, or rice over the glue. When the glue is dry, invite students to cut apart the quarters to make cards. Ask students to choose a partner. Have partners close their eyes, and challenge the students to guess their partner's words by tracing them with their fingers. Invite students to copy the words in their word bank for letter formation and memorization.

CLOUDY WORDS

materials

cotton balls

large sheets of blue
construction paper

crayons or markers

glue

Place cotton balls, large sheets of blue construction paper, crayons or markers, and glue in a learning center. Invite a small group of students to sit at the center. Have each student choose a word from the word wall. Ask students to share their word with the group, and invite them to write their word in the air three times with their index finger. Invite each student to print his or her word on construction paper. Have students trace over the letters with glue and lay cotton balls over the glue until the entire word is covered. Challenge students to write a sentence on their paper and underline their sight word. Then invite students to draw a picture to go with their sentence. Collect all the "cloudy" words, and put them together to make a class book. Place the book in a reading center for students to read on their own time. Students can touch the cloudy words as they read the book.

ALUMINUM-FOIL WORDS

materials

large pieces of cardboard

glue

yarn

aluminum foil

masking tape

permanent markers
(assorted colors)

word bank

Invite each student to choose a word from the word wall. Give each student a large piece of cardboard, glue, yarn, and a sheet of aluminum foil. Invite students to write their word on their piece of cardboard with a pencil. Ask students to trace the word with glue. Have students lay yarn on the glue and press down firmly. Allow time for the glue to completely dry. Have students cover their cardboard and yarn with a sheet of aluminum foil. Ask students to turn the cardboard over and secure the foil with masking tape. Invite students to mold the foil around the yarn. Have students use a permanent black marker to outline their raised word and assorted colors of permanent markers to color around their word. Invite students to close their eyes and touch their word with their fingers. Have students trade their words with classmates and touch the word with their eyes closed. As students feel each letter, have them write it in their word bank.

SAND-PAINTING WORDS

materials

sand

baby-food jars

powdered tempera paint

glue

pieces of cardboard

word bank

In advance, collect sand and place it in several baby-food jars. Make an assortment of colors by adding a spoonful of powdered tempera paint to each jar. Invite each student to choose a sight word from the word wall. Give each student jars of colored sand, glue, and a piece of cardboard. Invite students to write their word on their piece of cardboard. Ask them to trace their word with glue and then sprinkle small amounts of colored sand on top of the glue. Invite students to use the glue and colored sand to add additional designs around their word. When the glue is dry, invite students to touch each letter of their word. As students touch each letter, invite them to write it in their word bank. Place the colored sand, glue, and cardboard in a learning center so students can repeat the activity with different sight words.

PIPE-CLEANER WORDS

materials

large index cards

pipe cleaners

word bank

In advance, write several sight words on separate large index cards to make word cards. Working with a small group of students, distribute a handful of pipe cleaners to each student. Invite students to listen very closely while you say a sight word. Challenge students to use the pipe cleaners to form all of the letters they hear. Display the word card, and invite students to use their pipe cleaners to add or change the letters they need to spell the sight word. Ask students to record the word in their word bank. Repeat the activity with a different sight word.

WORDS OF CLAY

materials

clay

waxed paper

word bank

plastic resealable bags

Cornmeal Clay Recipe

1½ cups (375 ml) flour
1½ cups (375 ml) cornmeal
1 cup (250 ml) salt
1 cup (250 ml) water

Mix together all the ingredients in a bowl. Add more water as needed for a dough-like consistency. Store in an airtight container or a plastic resealable bag. Clay will keep for at least a month.

Place cornmeal clay or commercial clay in a learning center. Invite a small group of students to sit at the center. Invite each student to choose a word from the word wall. Distribute to each student a lump of clay and a piece of waxed paper to use as a work surface. Invite students to form their word on their waxed paper in two different ways (e.g., long and skinny, short and fat). Next, encourage them to say their word in a sentence and then record it on the How about a Try page of their word bank. Challenge students to use their clay to make other words from the word wall. Students can store their clay in a plastic resealable bag.

PEANUT-BUTTER WORDS

Peanut-Butter Clay Recipe

1 cup (250 ml) smooth peanut butter
1 cup (250 ml) honey
2 cups (500 ml) powdered milk

materials

peanut-butter clay

waxed paper

chart paper

Mix all ingredients in a bowl until you get a dough-like consistency. If necessary, add more powdered milk to make the clay more manageable.

Invite a small group of students to sit at a learning center. Have students help you make the peanut-butter clay. Distribute a lump of clay and a piece of waxed paper to each student. Invite students to touch, smell, and taste their clay. Challenge students to brainstorm a sentence about their clay (e.g., *We mixed the honey with the peanut butter, We used a spoon to mix the ingredients,* or *The clay tasted good*). Record their sentences on chart paper, and underline any sight words. Invite students to silently read each sentence. When they come to an underlined sight word, invite them to form the word using their clay. After the students have formed all the sight words, they can eat their yummy clay.

COOKIE-DOUGH WORDS

materials

Who Took the Cookies from the Cookie Jar? by Rozanne Lanczak Williams (Creative Teaching Press)

sentence strips

scissors

plastic resealable bags

cookie dough

waxed paper

baking sheets

oven

In advance, write on sentence strips each sentence from the picture book *Who Took the Cookies from the Cookie Jar?* Underline each sight word (e.g., *who, took, the, left, from, me, yes, you, not,* and *then*). Cut each sentence strip into separate word cards, and put all the cards for each sentence into a separate plastic resealable bag. Invite a small group of students to sit at a learning center. Read aloud the story, and then give each student a plastic bag of word cards. Ask students to read the words in their bag and arrange their words to form a sentence from the story. Once all sentences have been arranged, invite the students to put all the sentences in order to retell the story. Distribute a lump of cookie dough and a piece of waxed paper to each student. Invite students to use the cookie dough to form an underlined sight word from their sentence on their waxed paper. Ask students to place their cookie-dough word on a baking sheet, and bake the dough. Give students their baked cookie. Reread the story. As students hear their word being used in the story, they can take a bite of their cookie word.

WORDS SPELL RELIEF

Salt Dough Recipe
1 cup (250 ml) flour
¼ cup (50 ml) salt
⅓ cup (85 ml) water

materials

salt dough

index cards

heavy cardboard

toothpicks

assorted colors of
tempera paint

paintbrushes

Make clay by combining flour, salt, and water in a large bowl. Knead clay for consistency.

In advance, make salt dough. Choose several sight words, and write each word on a separate index card. Distribute to each student a word card, a lump of dough, and a piece of heavy cardboard to use as a base. Have students use their dough to shape each letter of their word. Ask students to pinch the dough with their fingers to add texture to their word or use toothpicks to add designs. Allow time for the dough to dry, and then invite students to paint their dough. Share students' work as part of a sight word art display, or place the words in a learning center so students can use them as a tactile resource.

SIMON SAYS

materials

large index cards

Write several sight words on separate large index cards to make word cards. Display the word cards, and have students practice clapping and chanting the spelling of each word before playing the game. Display the words in a variety of places around the classroom (e.g., chair, door, desk). Invite a volunteer to perform an action as he or she finds one of the words. For example, say *Amy, Simon says find the word* with *and clap three times* or *Thomas, Simon says find the word* when *and hop on one foot in a circle while spelling the word.* If the student finds the word and performs the action correctly, invite him or her to choose a new word and give the next instruction to a classmate. If the student does not perform the action correctly or goes to the wrong word, encourage him or her to try again.

HOPSCOTCH WORDS

materials

chalk

beanbags

In advance, use chalk to draw several hopscotch games on pavement or asphalt. Print a separate sight word in each hopscotch square. Divide the class into small groups. Invite a student from each group to toss a beanbag on a word. Have the student hop from square to square and say the word in each square. When the player lands on the word with the beanbag, have the student pick it up and continue hopping to the end of the hopscotch squares. Invite the student to return, hopping and chanting the spelling of the word that had the beanbag. Have another student from each group repeat the game with a different sight word.

SWAT!

materials

2 plastic flyswatters

Write a list of several sight words on the chalkboard twice. Practice saying the words with students before beginning the game. Divide the class into two teams. Give the first person on each team a flyswatter, and have the two team representatives stand in front of the chalkboard. Say a sentence aloud that includes one of the sight words. The first player to lay his or her flyswatter on the correct word on the chalkboard scores a point for his or her team. Have the scoring player record the point in a tally column for his or her team, and ask both players to hand their flyswatters to the next players. The game continues until one team reaches ten points.

BEAT THE CLOCK

materials

large sheets of construction paper

obstacle items (e.g., milk or juice cartons, cardboard boxes, wooden blocks, plastic buckets, broom or mop handles, hula hoops, desks, chairs, pillows, books)

masking tape

timer or stopwatch

Copy several sight words on separate large sheets of construction paper to make large word cards. Set up an obstacle course in the classroom. Choose actions for the students to do in the obstacle course, such as jump over a milk carton, crawl under a desk, and run along a taped line. Tape a word card to each obstacle in the course. Practice saying each word with students as you demonstrate how to go through the obstacle course. Invite a student to go through the obstacle course. Set a timer or stopwatch for one minute, and have the student shout each word as he or she completes each obstacle. Once the minute is up, invite the student to write each word he or she shouted on the chalkboard and ask the class to clap and spell each word. Invite a new player to run the course.

BODY-BUILDING WORDS

materials

index cards

Choose several sight words, and write each word on an index card to make word cards. Divide your class into small groups, and distribute a different word card to each group. Explain that each group must use their bodies to form their word. Tell students they may stand, sit, or lie down. Invite each group to practice before you take the class to an open space in the classroom or on the playground. Have each group build their word, and invite the rest of the class to guess the word. Continue the activity until all groups have had a chance to share their "body-building" word with the class.

SIGHT-WORD SHUFFLE

materials

chart paper

word bank

Write the five vowels vertically on chart paper. Ask students to suggest a movement to correspond with each vowel (e.g., *a = stomp feet, e = snap*). Write the movement for each vowel on the chart paper. Choose a word from the word wall, and write it on the chalkboard. Have students write the word in the air three times using their index finger. Invite students to use the movements for each vowel to spell the word. For example, to spell *began*, have students say *b*, *e* (snap), *g*, *a* (stomp feet), *n*. Repeat the activity with a different sight word. Ask students to record words in their word bank.

JITTERBUG DANCE

materials

word bank

Discuss with students how letters of the alphabet can be sorted into "high," "middle," and "low" letters. For example, *h* and *l* are considered high letters, the letters *a* and *c* middle letters, and the letters *g* and *y* are low letters. Divide your chalkboard into three sections. Label each section with the categories *High Letters, Middle Letters,* and *Low Letters.* Starting with the letter *a,* decide as a class which category each letter will go in. Invite a student to write the letter *a* under the correct category. Repeat this until all the letters of the alphabet have been placed in the correct category. Explain to students that for each letter category there is a specific movement. For example, for the high letters have students stretch their body as high as they can and clap above their head. For middle letters, have students bend their knees slightly and clap. For low letters, have students squat down in a low position and clap close to their feet. Invite students to practice the movements with several letters. Choose a sight word, and write it on the chalkboard. Practice saying the word with the students. Challenge students to incorporate the movements as they call out each letter of the word. Repeat the word and motions three times. Ask students to record the word in their word bank. Repeat the activity with a different word.

WATER WORDS

materials

index cards

paintbrushes

small cups of water

In advance, write several sight words on separate index cards to make word cards. Take the class to an open area of pavement. Distribute a word card, a paintbrush, and a small cup of water to each student. Invite students to dip their paintbrush in the water and write their sight word three or more times on the pavement. Challenge students to paint a sentence that includes their word. Ask students to repeat the activity with a different word.

GOOEY WORDS

materials

plastic resealable bags

hairstyling gel or finger paint

masking tape

tagboard

Fill a plastic resealable bag with hairstyling gel or finger paint for each student. Use masking tape to secure each bag to a piece of tagboard. Invite students to choose a word from the word wall and use one finger to press the letters of their word into the gel or paint. Students can erase their word by gently rubbing the bag with the palm of their hand until it is evenly distributed inside the bag.

FINGER-PAINTING FUN

Finger Paint Recipe
½ cup (125 ml) liquid starch
½ cup (125 ml) water
½ cup (125 ml) tempera paint

materials

finger paint

paper plates

black construction paper

sentence strips

Mix all ingredients in a bowl for a paint-like consistency.

In advance, make finger paint or use commercial paint, and place it on a paper plate for each student. Invite each student to choose a word from the word wall. Distribute black construction paper, finger paint, and several sentence strips to each student. Challenge students to finger-paint their word again and again, one word next to the other in several colors on their construction paper. Next, encourage students to finger-paint a sentence that includes their sight word on a sentence strip. Display students' work as part of a bulletin board display. For extra fun, place the paintings and strips in a learning center, so students can match the strips to the paintings.

WRITE IT WITH SAND

In a learning center, place a tub or pan of wet sand on a table covered with newspaper. Invite each student to choose several words from the word wall. Have students practice writing their words in the sand with their fingers. Challenge students to write sentences with their words in the sand. Students can erase their words or sentences by rubbing the sand with the palm of their hand until the sand becomes smooth.

materials

tub or pan of wet sand

newspaper

PUDDING PLAY

materials

index card

masking tape

jar with lid

packages of instant pudding
(1 package per 10 children)

milk

sentence strips

paper plates

pocket chart

spoons

Invite a small group of students to sit in a circle on the floor. Write a sight word on the chalkboard. Practice clapping and chanting the spelling of the word with the students. Invite students to observe as you print the word on an index card. Tape the index card to a jar. Make instant pudding by following the directions on the package. Invite student volunteers to pour the ingredients into the jar, secure the lid, and pass the jar of pudding around the circle. Ask each student to shake the jar to mix the ingredients. Challenge students to use the word in a sentence as they shake the jar. Record each sentence on a sentence strip, and underline the sight word. Have students continue to pass the jar until each student has used the word in a sentence. Pour a generous amount of pudding onto a paper plate for each student. Put all the sentence strips in a pocket chart. Practice reading and saying the sentences with the students. As children see and hear the underlined word in each sentence, have them write the word in their pudding with their fingers. After they write the sight word from each sentence, invite them to eat their pudding.

We will eat pudding.

I will mix the pudding.

Mrs. Crosby will help us.

A DASH OF SALT

materials

salt

water

small paper cups

black construction paper

medicine droppers

index cards

In advance, make a salt solution by dissolving 1 teaspoon (5 ml) of salt in 2 table-spoons (30 ml) of water in small paper cups. Place the salt solution, black construction paper, and medicine droppers in a learning center. Invite a small group of students to sit at the learning center. Write several sight words on separate index cards, and distribute a word card to each student. Have students write their word with their index finger in the air three times and underline it each time. Invite students to use the salt solution and a medicine dropper to write their word on construction paper. Encourage students to use the salt solution to add designs and borders to their paper. The students will only see water at first, but when the water evaporates, glistening salt will appear on their paper.

SCRAMBLED WORDS

materials

overhead transparency,
projector, and markers

shaving cream

In advance, write a list of sentences that each include a scrambled sight word on an overhead transparency. Underline the scrambled word in each sentence (e.g., *The cars went <u>drune</u> the bridge*). Working with a small group of students, place a generous amount of shaving cream on each child's desk. Have students spread out their shaving cream over their entire work area. Place the transparency on an overhead projector. Invite a student to read a sentence aloud. Challenge students to unscramble the underlined word and write it correctly in their shaving cream. Ask students to raise their hand to share the unscrambled word. Repeat the activity with a new sentence and scrambled word.

STAMP IT!

materials

rubber letter stamps

construction paper

assorted colors of ink pads

glue

Place several rubber letter stamps, construction paper, and ink pads in a learning center. Invite a small group of students to each choose a sight word from the word wall. Challenge students to use the rubber stamps and ink pads to stamp their word on paper again and again in as many different color combinations as possible. Encourage students to use the stamps to create colorful borders. Frame student work by gluing each creation to colored construction paper. Attach finished work to a bulletin board titled *Stamping out Sight Words*. For extra fun, encourage students to stamp sentences that include sight words.

RAINBOW COLORS

Make "glue paint" in each color of the rainbow by adding a spoonful of dry tempera paint to separate glue bottles. Place large sheets of construction paper and the glue paint at a learning center. Ask a small group of students to come to the learning center, and invite each student to choose a word from the word wall. Challenge students to use each color of the glue paint to write their word on a sheet of construction paper. Invite students to repeat the activity with a new word from the word wall. When the glue is dry, share students' work as part of a bulletin board display titled *A Rainbow of Words*. Students can touch the glue words for a visual and tactile resource.

MAGNETIC MADNESS

Place several magnetic boards and letters in a learning center. Invite a small group of students to sit at the learning center. Choose a sight word, and say it aloud. Teach the group to echo the word back. After you and the students echo back and forth several times, invite each student to use the magnetic letters to form the word on a magnetic board. Write the word on the chalkboard so students can check and change their answer if necessary. Invite students to record the correctly spelled sight word in their word bank.

STRING ALONG

materials

index cards

large pieces of yarn

word bank

sentence strips

Write several sight words on separate index cards to make word cards. Working with a small group of students, distribute a word card and several large pieces of yarn to each student. Invite a volunteer to read his or her word aloud to the group. Challenge the other students to form the word using their yarn. Have the volunteer display his or her word card so the other students can check their work. Ask students to record the word in their word bank. Continue until all students have shared their word with the group. As an extension, invite students to write a sentence with their sight word on a sentence strip. Ask students to underline the sight word. Place the yarn and sentence strips in a learning center so students can use the yarn to form the underlined word on each sentence strip.

PRETZEL MODELS

materials

index cards

pretzel sticks

marshmallows or cheese cubes

plastic resealable bags

large sheets of butcher paper

In advance, write several sight words on index cards to make word cards. Place a handful of pretzel sticks and marshmallows or cheese cubes into a plastic resealable bag for each student. Distribute a word card and a plastic resealable bag to each student. Challenge students to push their pretzel sticks into the cheese cubes or marshmallows to make a model of their word. Distribute more pretzel sticks and cheese cubes or marshmallows as needed. Invite students to place their pretzel words on butcher paper for a display. Challenge them to say their pretzel word in a sentence to the class. After each pretzel word has been used in a sentence, invite students to eat their model.

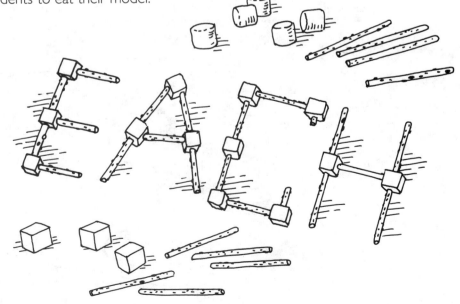

SECRET WORDS

materials

Alphabet Cards reproducibles (pages 66–68)

scissors

plastic resealable bags

Photocopy two sets of Alphabet Cards for each student. Give each student the sets of cards, and have students cut them apart. Write a group of sight words on the chalkboard. Practice saying the words with the students. Tell students that one of the words is a "secret" word. Choose a word from the chalkboard, and say each one of its letters in random order. Have students find the corresponding card for each letter and arrange the letters in the order they were said. Have students look at the sight words on the chalkboard to decide which is the secret word. Invite students to rearrange the letters to identify the secret word. Invite students to raise their hand and share the secret word. Continue the game with other sight words from the chalkboard. Have students store their cards in a plastic resealable bag.

SOAKING UP SIGHT WORDS

materials

sponge letters

tempera paint

paper plates

large sheets of construction paper

Place sponge letters, paint on paper plates, and large sheets of construction paper in a learning center. Invite a small group of students to sit at the learning center. Have each student choose three or more words from the word wall. Challenge students to sponge-paint their words on their sheet of paper. For extra fun, invite students to sponge-paint sentences using the sight words. When the paint is dry, display students' work as part of a bulletin board display. Students can repeat the activity with new words.

MAKING IT TWICE

materials

base-ten rods and unit cubes

word bank

Invite students to use base-ten rods and unit cubes to form sight words from the word wall. Challenge students to build their words in lowercase letters and then in uppercase letters. Invite students to record their words in their word bank. Place the materials in a learning center so students can practice building more words on their own.

SNACKING ON SIGHT WORDS

materials

snacks (e.g., pretzel sticks, cereal, chocolate chips, marshmallows, nuts, raisins)

paper plates

Place an assortment of snacks and paper plates in a learning center. Invite a small group of students to sit at a learning center. Ask each student to choose a word from the word wall. Challenge students to use the snack items to form their word on a paper plate. After students are done forming their word, challenge each student to say a word and use it in a sentence. After they have used their word in a sentence, invite students to eat their yummy word. Invite students to repeat the activity with a different word.

COOTIE!

materials

paper strips

paper bag

Write several sight words on individual paper strips and place them in a paper bag. Invite a student to select a paper strip from the bag. Write only one or two letters of the word on the chalkboard, and write blank lines for the remaining letters. Challenge students to take turns guessing what the missing letters are. If a student correctly chooses a letter, write the letter in the correct space. When a child guesses a letter not in the word, begin drawing one part of an insect on the chalkboard. For each incorrect guess, draw an insect's head, abdomen, thorax, six legs (one at a time), and two antennae (one at a time). The object of the game is for players to guess the word before you draw the whole insect. Invite students to take turns choosing words from the paper bag and drawing the insect.

COLOR ME FANCY

materials

construction paper

stencils

art supplies (e.g., crayons or markers, scissors, paint/paint-brushes, beads, feathers, ribbons, pasta, beans, sequins, glitter, glue)

Place construction paper, stencils, and art supplies at a learning center. Ask a small group of students to come to the learning center. Invite each student to choose a word from the word wall. Invite students to use stencils to trace their word on construction paper. Invite students to decorate the inside of their word with a variety of art materials. Frame each student's creation on a piece of colorful construction paper. Display the finished work on a bulletin board so students can use the words as a resource in their reading and writing. Students can repeat the activity with a different sight word.

DIAL A WORD

materials

Telephone reproducible
(page 69)

Give each student a photocopy of the Telephone reproducible. Choose ten sight words, and write on the chalkboard a 1-800 word for each one (e.g., *1-800-when* or *1-800-because*). Challenge students to translate each word into a telephone number using the phone keys on their telephone sheet and record each number on their sheet. Have students exchange papers with a partner and "translate" the numbers back into the original sight words by using the keys on their telephone sheet. As an extension, invite students to prepare their own 1-800 words for a classmate to translate into a 1-800 number. For extra fun, students can also calculate the "value" of the words (e.g., *when* is worth a value of 9 + 4 + 3 + 6 = 22). For extra fun, students can use play phones to punch in numbers to translate each word into a number.

"SUN"SATIONAL WORD MOBILES

materials

Mobile reproducible
(page 70)

Suns reproducible
(page 71)

clothes hangers

crayons or markers

yarn

scissors

hole punch

Give each student a photocopy of the Mobile and the Suns reproducibles, a clothes hanger, crayons or markers, and several pieces of yarn. Invite students to color and cut out their mobile pattern. Have them punch two holes in the top of their mobile pattern, thread yarn through the holes, and tie the yarn to the top portion of their hanger. Each time students learn a new sight word, have them write the word on a separate sun pattern. Ask students to color and cut out their sun pattern and then punch a hole through the top of their sun and the bottom of their mobile. Have students thread a piece of yarn through the holes and tie the ends. As students learn new sight words, they can keep adding them to their mobiles. Hang the mobiles from the ceiling so students can use them as a reading and writing resource.

EVAPORATING WORDS

wet sponge

paper fan

paper

Use a wet sponge to write a sight word on the chalkboard. Invite a student to make the word evaporate by waving a paper fan by the wet word as fast as possible. Meanwhile, invite the other students to write the word on a piece of paper as many times as they can until the word has evaporated off the chalkboard. Call out *Evaporation* when the word has completely disappeared from the chalkboard, and ask all students to stop writing. Invite students to share how many times they wrote the word correctly. Play again with a new sight word.

GRAB-BAG GUESS

materials

Alphabet Cards reproducibles
(pages 66–68)

scissors

pocket chart

paper strips

paper bag

Photocopy one set of Alphabet Cards. Cut out the cards, and display them in a pocket chart. Write several sight words on separate paper strips. Fold the strips in half, and put them in a paper bag. Invite a volunteer to choose a slip from the bag and tell his or her classmates how many letters are in the word. Next, invite the student to describe the first letter of the word. For example, for the letter *a* he or she might say *The first letter is round and has a small tail.* Have students look at their cards to find the letter that meets that description. Invite students to raise their hand and guess the letter. Have the student who correctly guessed the letter write it on the chalkboard. If the guessed letter is incorrect, invite students to keep guessing until the letter is revealed. Invite the student who guessed correctly to describe the next letter of the same word. Encourage students to use the word wall for reference. Continue the game until the word has been revealed. Repeat the game with a different sight word.

SHAPING UP SIGHT WORDS

materials

word bank

In advance, write several sight words on one side of the chalkboard and trace the outer shape of each word. On the other side of the chalkboard, draw the same shapes in random order, this time without the words. Practice saying the words with the class. Invite a volunteer to match a word with its shape by writing the correct word in its shape. Continue the activity until each shape has been filled with the correct sight word. Invite students to practice writing the words in their word bank. For extra fun, challenge students to draw on paper the outer shapes for three or more words. Invite students to exchange their paper with a partner and solve each other's puzzles.

BUGGED OVER WORDS

materials

Creepy Crawlers reproducible (page 72)

pipe cleaners

art supplies (i.e., sequins, ribbons, "wiggle eyes," scissors, glue)

picture books

Give each student a photocopy of the Creepy Crawlers reproducible, pipe cleaners, and art supplies. Write four sight words on the chalkboard, and practice saying the words with the class. Invite students to write the four words on their Creepy Crawlers sheet. Invite students to make a "bug word searcher." Have them make a loop with the end of a pipe cleaner and tie on six pipe cleaners for legs and two for antennae. Encourage students to use sequins and ribbons to decorate their bug word searcher, and glue a wiggle eye at the end of each antenna. Demonstrate how to use the bug word searcher to scan text and locate sight words. Invite students to read picture books and use their bug word searcher to locate words on their sheet. Invite students to record on their Creepy Crawlers sheet the number of times they find each word in the books they are reading.

EXTRA! EXTRA!

materials

index cards

paper

scissors

glue

magazines or other
printed materials

Write several sight words on index cards to make word cards. Distribute to each student a word card, paper, scissors, glue, and a magazine or other printed materials. Invite students to locate and circle their sight word in the printed materials. When students have located several examples of their word in different fonts and sizes, invite them to cut out the words. Challenge students to glue their words on their paper to make a collage. Place the materials in a learning center, and encourage students to make more collages using different sight words. Display students' work as part of a bulletin board display.

WORDS HAVE VALUE

materials

paper

Write the entire alphabet across the chalkboard. Below the letters, starting with *a*, write the numbers 1–26. Continue this until all letters have been assigned a number. Write several sight words on the chalkboard, and practice clapping and chanting the spelling of each word with the class. Distribute paper to each student. Challenge students to figure out the value of each sight word (e.g., *all: a=1, l=12, l=12 so all=25*). Invite students to share which word had the highest value and which word had the least value. Discuss with students any similarities or differences they noticed with the group of words. Repeat the activity with different sight words. To extend learning, invite students to choose different sight words from the word wall and figure out their value.

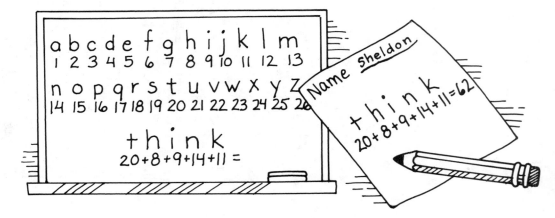

WHO AM I?

materials

Choose a word from the word wall, such as *what*, without sharing the word with the class. Write on the chalkboard four clues that describe the word (e.g., *I have four letters. I begin with* wh. *I have the vowel a in me. I rhyme with* nut). Invite volunteers to read the clues one at a time. Explain to students that they are to look at the word wall to find the word that matches the clues and then raise their hand when they want to make a guess. Repeat the activity using new words and clues. For an extension, have students brainstorm clues for new words.

WORDS ON THE DOOR

materials

index cards

construction paper

crayons or markers

Write several sight words on index cards to make word cards. Distribute a word card and a sheet of construction paper to each student. Invite students to write their word in the air three times with their index finger and underline the word each time. Invite students to use crayons or markers to write and decorate their word on their paper. Collect students' papers, and display several of them on a classroom door. Tell students that each time they leave the classroom they need to read and spell the words on the door. Change the words on the door weekly.

CODED WORDS

materials

Symbols reproducible
(page 73)

Use the Symbols reproducible to write several sight words on the chalkboard in "code." Tell students that each symbol stands for a letter and the letters spell a sight word. Give each student a photocopy of the Symbols reproducible. Invite students to use the symbols to decode the sight words and write them on their sheet. For extra fun, invite students to come up with their own coded words. Have students exchange papers and decode a classmate's words.

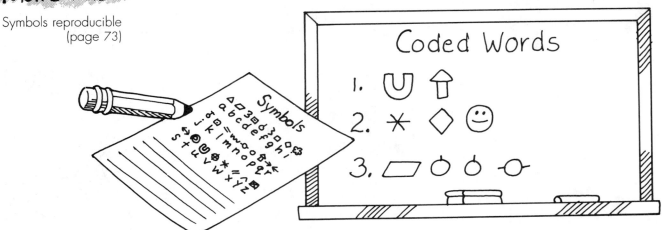

GUESS WHO

materials

index cards

masking tape

In advance, write several sight words on index cards to make word cards. Tape a word card to each student's back. Have the students walk around the room and ask each other *yes* and *no* questions to discover which word is on their back. When students correctly guess the word on their card, they move the cards to their shirt front and continue answering other students' questions.

WORD DETECTIVES

materials

Word Search reproducible
(page 74)

Photocopy the Word Search reproducible, and write several sight words on the grid horizontally, vertically, or diagonally. Write random letters in the empty squares to hide the words. Give each student a photocopy of the completed word search. Write the words students need to search for on the chalkboard. Practice saying the words with the class. Challenge students to find and circle the words on their word search. Each time students find a word, have them write it on their paper. To extend learning, have students create their own word search with sight words. Students can exchange their word search with a classmate.

THE JOLLY POSTMAN

materials

Postcard reproducible
(page 75)

crayons or markers

word bank

Give each student a photocopy of the Postcard reproducible. Challenge students to use sight words to write a message on the postcard to a classmate. Invite students to illustrate the front of their postcard. Ask students to address their postcard to their classmate and deliver it. Invite classmates to read their postcard and circle any words in the message they see on the word wall. Have students record the sight words in their word bank. Invite students to share their postcard and the sight words with the class. Place more Postcard reproducibles and crayons or markers in a learning center. Encourage students to use sight words to write back to their classmates.

RICH WITH WORDS

materials

construction paper

stapler

crayons or markers

index cards

In advance, invite each student to make a "word wallet." Have students fold a sheet of construction paper in half lengthwise and then into thirds. Help them securely staple the folds. Invite students to use crayons or markers to decorate their wallet and print *Rich with Words* on it. Each time students are introduced to new sight words, have them add some "money" (words) to their wallet. Have the students use crayons or markers to write sight words on index cards. Challenge them to decorate the cards to look like dollar bills. Have students place the cards in their wallet. Invite students to practice reading their cards whenever they wish. Each week, invite students to add words to their wallet. Encourage them to read their wallet at least once a week to review old and new words. Ask volunteers to show and read their words to the class. Once a month, invite students to read their words to you. Keep a record of the words missed or mastered on each student's Sight Words Record Sheet (page 62). At the end of the month, ask students to clean out their wallet and start over with new words.

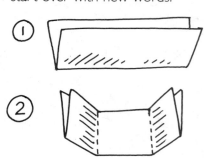

CHAIN OF WORDS

materials

3" x 12" (7.5 cm x 30.5 cm) paper strips

crayons or markers

glue

Distribute 3" x 12" (7.5 cm x 30.5 cm) paper strips and crayons or markers to each student. Each time students are introduced to a new sight word, have them write it on a paper strip. On a separate strip, have students write a sentence with the sight word. Invite students to glue together the ends of each strip and link the strips to create a chain. Ask student volunteers to show and read their chain to the class. Have students link the chains together to form a class chain. Display the chain around the classroom. Each week, invite students to add new sight words to the chain. Encourage students to read the chain at least once a week to review old and new words. Have students keep adding new words to the class chain. Students can use the chain as a reading and writing resource. For variation, students can make their own word chain by linking the individual letters of a sight word together. Students can wear it as a necklace.

EAT MY WORDS

materials

Word Makers reproducible
(page 76)

Eat My Words reproducible
(page 77)

scissors

paper bag

box of alphabet cereal

In advance, photocopy the Word Makers reproducible, and write a sight word in each rectangle. Cut the rectangles apart, and place them in a paper bag. Photocopy the Eat My Words reproducible for each student. Put the reproducibles and a box of alphabet cereal in a learning center. Invite a small group of students to sit at the center. Give each student an Eat My Words reproducible, and invite each student to choose a sight word from the paper bag. Have students place their word in the first column of their sheet. Next, have students use alphabet cereal to build their word in the second column. In the last column, invite students to write their word. Have students repeat this process until they have completed their sheet. Have them choose a classmate to check their work, and then invite them to eat their cereal words.

VESTED WORDS

materials

paper grocery bags

art supplies (e.g., crayons or markers, scissors, paint/paintbrushes, beads, feathers, ribbons, pasta, beans, sequins, glitter)

glue

word bank

Distribute to each student a paper grocery bag and art supplies to make a vest. Have students push out the sides of their bag and lay it flat. Ask students to cut out two armholes and a neckhole. Have students turn the bag to the front side and cut a straight line (in the top layer only) from the bottom of the bag to the neckhole. Invite students to decorate their "vest" with the art supplies. Each time students are introduced to new sight words, have them write the words on their vest. Each week, encourage students to add words to their vest. Invite students to read their vest at least once a week to review old and new words. Challenge students to read the words to you or a partner. Students can practice writing the words in their word bank.

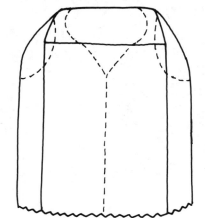

BELTS AND BRACELETS

materials

index cards

tagboard

art supplies (e.g., crayons or markers, paint/paintbrushes, beads, feathers, ribbons, pasta, beans, sequins, glitter, scissors)

hole punch

yarn

construction-paper strips

glue

In advance, choose several sight words, and write them on separate index cards to make word cards. Distribute to each student a word card, tagboard, and art supplies. Have students write their word in large print on their tagboard and decorate it. Ask students to punch a hole at each end of their tagboard, thread a piece of yarn through each hole, and tie it off. Invite students to tie their tagboard around their waist like a belt. Distribute several construction-paper strips to each student. Encourage students to share their belt with their classmates, and as they share, challenge classmates to write a sentence on a paper strip using the sight word on the belt. Have students place the strip around their wrist and glue the ends to make a bracelet. Challenge students to collect as many sentence bracelets as possible. Have students read their bracelets to you or a partner.

WORDY HEADBANDS

materials

sentence strips

art supplies (e.g., crayons or markers, paint/paintbrushes, beads, feathers, ribbons, pasta, beans, sequins, glitter)

glue, tape, or stapler

index cards

Choose several sight words from the word wall, and write each word on a separate sentence strip. Write the same words on the chalkboard. Give each student a sentence strip and art supplies. Invite students to decorate their sentence strip and make a headband by joining the ends of their sentence strip with glue, tape, or staples. Invite students to wear their headband. Give each student five index cards. Ask each student to choose five sight words from the chalkboard and write a sentence with each word on a separate index card. Challenge students to find the classmates who wrote a sentence with the word on their headband. If students find a classmate with their word in a sentence, have them place the card in their headband. Invite students to share their collected sentences with the class or a partner.

BINGO

materials

Bingo reproducible
(page 78)

counters (beans, buttons,
pennies, etc.)

Give each student a photocopy of the Bingo reproducible. To prepare the game, have students write words from the word wall in random squares on their Bingo card. Distribute counters to students. Choose a volunteer to call words in random order from the word wall, and write each word on the chalkboard. When students find a word on their card, have them cover it with a counter. When a player covers a row horizontally, diagonally, or vertically, invite him or her to call out *Sight Words*. Invite the winner to read and spell the words to the caller. If all his or her words were called, he or she becomes the new caller. Invite students to clear their card to play again.

CONCENTRATION

materials

index cards

Choose several sight words, and write them on the chalkboard. Practice chanting and spelling the words with the class. Distribute several index cards to each student, and invite students to write each word from the chalkboard on a separate card. Ask students to choose a partner and combine their cards together so that there are two cards of each word. Invite students to turn the cards facedown, mix them up, and spread them out. Invite the first player to turn over two cards. If the cards match, the player keeps the cards. If the cards are not a match, the player turns them back over. Play continues with the next player choosing two cards. Invite students to keep playing until all matching pairs have been found. The player with the most matches wins the game.

GRAPH IT

materials

Graph It reproducible
(page 79)

writing paper

timer or clock

Give each student a photocopy of the Graph It reproducible and writing paper. Ask students to work in pairs. Have each pair choose a word from the word wall. Set a timer or watch a clock for one minute. Challenge the students to write their word as many times as they can in one minute. After the minute is up, invite students to trade papers, check the paper for correct spelling, and then return it to their partner. Invite students to graph how many times they spelled the sight word correctly in one minute. Challenge students to increase the number on their graph while playing again with the same word. When students have reached the end of their graph, invite them to repeat the activity with a new sight word.

PUZZLED TO PIECES

materials

index cards

large sheets of
construction paper

crayons or markers

scissors

plastic resealable bags

Write several sight words on index cards, and invite each student to choose a card. Distribute large sheets of construction paper and crayons or markers to each student. Have students write their word on the construction paper and decorate around it. Challenge students to turn their paper facedown and draw a puzzle on the blank side. Invite students to cut apart their puzzle and put it back together to form their word. Have students take apart their puzzle and store the pieces in a plastic resealable bag. Collect all the puzzles, and place them in a learning center. Invite a small group of students to sit at a learning center. Have each student put together several different puzzles.

COVER ALL

materials

permanent marker

wooden or foam cubes

index cards

counters (coins, beans, pasta, etc.)

Make letter dice by using a permanent marker to write a letter of the alphabet on each side of 1" (2.5 cm) wooden or foam cubes. Choose several sight words, and write them on separate index cards. Place word cards, letter dice, and counters in a learning center. Invite a small group of students to sit at the center. Invite each student to choose a word card. Invite the first player to roll the letter dice. If the dice show a letter found on the player's word card, have the player place a counter over the same letter on his or her card. Have students take turns rolling and covering letters until one player covers his or her entire word card. The player with the card covered first is the winner. Have students choose new word cards and play again.

FIND A WORD

materials

index cards

envelopes

Invite each student to choose a sight word from the word wall. Distribute several index cards and an envelope to each student, and have students write each letter of their word on a separate index card. Ask students to put their cards in their envelope and write their name on the front of their envelope. Collect all the envelopes, and hide them throughout the classroom. Challenge students to find the "lost" envelopes in the classroom. When they find an envelope, invite them to put the word back together and return the envelope to the owner. Encourage students to keep searching for lost envelopes until all have been returned.

A GIFT OF WORDS

materials

index cards

masking tape

small gift-wrapped box

cassette/cassette player

In advance, write several sight words on index cards to make word cards. Tape a word card to a small gift-wrapped box. Divide the class into two groups. Have one group form a circle and sit on the floor. Have the second group stand behind the first group. Play music and have students sitting on the floor quickly pass the gift box around the circle. Stop the music, and have the student holding the package spell the word and use it in a sentence. If he or she does this correctly, the person standing behind him or her joins the circle. The student who joins the circle sits and plays the game. If the student does not spell the word or use it correctly in a sentence, he or she stands behind a student sitting in the circle. The object of the game is to get everyone into the circle. Repeat the game with a different word.

IF YOU'RE READING

materials

chart paper (optional)

flyswatter

scissors

In advance, write the song "If You're Reading and You Know It" (below) on the chalkboard or chart paper. Cut out a rectangular hole in the center of a flyswatter so that when the flyswatter is placed over a word the word is framed. Choose several sight words, and write them on the chalkboard. Read the words with students. Invite students to choose a word from the board to use in the song "If You're Reading and You Know It." When you get to the part in the song that says "find the word," give the flyswatter to a student. Invite the student to come up to the board, find the word, and frame it with the flyswatter. Invite students to choose another word from the board. Sing the song again with the new word and have a different student frame the word on the chalkboard.

If You're Reading and You Know It

(sing to the tune of "If You're Happy and You Know It")

If you're reading and you know it say the word, **were, were.**
If you're reading and you know it say the word, **were, were.**
If you're reading and you know it and you really want to show it,
If you're reading and you know it say the word, **were, were.**

If you're reading and you know it find the word.
If you're reading and you know it find the word.
If you're reading and you know it and you really want to show it,
If you're reading and you know it find the word.

ADDITIONAL VERSES: Replace bolded words with other sight words.

1-2-3 SPELL THE WORD WITH ME!

materials

chart paper (optional)

large index cards

In advance, write the chant "1-2-3 Spell the Word with Me!" (below) on chart paper or the chalkboard. Write several letters of the alphabet on separate large index cards (some letters will need to be printed on more than one card). Distribute one card to each student. Choose a sight word, and write it on the chalkboard. Invite the students with the letter cards needed to spell the word to stand in the front of the class and arrange themselves in the correct order to spell the word. Have students say the chant aloud. When the chant asks for students to say the word, invite the class to shout the word. When the chant asks for students to spell the word, have them hold up the letter cards while the class shouts out each letter to spell the sight word. Repeat the activity with a new word. Write the word on the chalkboard, ask students to say the chant, and invite the class to determine who will sit down and who needs to come to the front of the room to spell the new word.

1-2-3 Spell the Word with Me!

1-2-3
Say the word with me!
1-2-3
Spell the word with me!

TELEPHONE

materials

Invite students to sit on the floor in a circle. Choose a sight word without sharing it with the group. Whisper the word and each letter to the student sitting next to you. Have that student then whisper the word and each letter to the student sitting next to him or her. Have each student in the circle repeat this until all students have had a turn to hear and whisper the word. Invite the last student in the circle to repeat aloud the word and the letters he or she heard. Then tell students the original word, and have them compare what they heard and said. Invite a student volunteer to choose a new word to start a new game.

ROLL AND SPELL

materials

ball

Have students sit in a circle. Choose a sight word, and roll a ball to a student as you say the word. The student who receives the ball says the first letter of the word then rolls the ball to another student. That student then says the next letter of the word. Invite students to continue rolling the ball until the sight word has been spelled. Have students continue the activity with new words until all students have had a turn.

STOP!

materials

Stop Sign reproducible
(page 80)

crayons or markers

craft sticks

scissors

glue

picture book

Give each student a photocopy of the Stop Sign reproducible, crayons or markers, and a craft stick. Ask students to color and cut out the stop sign and glue it to their craft stick. Write on the chalkboard a group of sight words from a picture book. Practice reading the words with the class. Tell students to hold up their stop sign each time they hear the word in the story. Read the story aloud. Invite a student volunteer to record on the chalkboard how many times students held up their stop sign for each word. After reading the story, discuss which words were used most and least. For an extension, use the data collected in the activity to make a class graph. Repeat the activity with a different story.

THE WORD IN THE WEB

materials

Alphabet Cards reproducibles
(pages 66–68)

chart paper (optional)

scissors

ball of yarn

In advance, write the lyrics for "The Word in the Web" (below) on chart paper or the chalkboard. Photocopy one set of Alphabet Cards, and cut them apart. Give each student a card. Invite students to sit in a circle and hold their card away from them so other students can see the letter. Choose a sight word, and say it aloud. Then sing the song with your class. When you get to the part where the spider gets a letter, toss a ball of yarn to the student who is holding the matching letter card. Have the class continue singing, and invite students to keep passing the yarn to the next student until the sight word is spelled and students have "spun a web." Challenge students to spin a web with a new sight word.

The Word in the Web

(sing to the tune of "The Farmer in the Dell")

The word in the web,
The word in the web,
Spider, spider, trap the word.
The word in the web.

The spider gets a **t.**
The spider gets a **t.**
Spider, spider, trap the word.
The spider gets a **t.**

The spider gets an **h.**
The spider gets an **h.**
Spider, spider, trap the word.
The spider gets an **h.**

The spider gets an **e.**
The spider gets an **e.**
Spider, spider, trap the word.
The spider gets an **e.**

The web spells **the.**
The web spells **the.**
Spider, spider, trapped the word.
The web spells **the.**

ADDITIONAL VERSES:

Replace the bolded letters and words with other letters and sight words.

WHERE'S THE WORD?

materials

chart paper (optional)

index cards

In advance, write the lyrics for "Where's the Word?"(below) on chart paper or the chalkboard. Choose several sight words, and write them on individual index cards. Distribute a word card to each student, and invite students to hold their card behind their back. Choose a sight word, and write it on the chalkboard. Then sing "Where's the Word?" with the class. Invite the student with the same word to respond to the questions in the song. Have that student stand up, show his or her word card, and spell the word to the class. Have students sing the song again with a new sight word.

Where's the Word?

(sing to the tune of "Are You Sleeping?")

Where's the word?
Where's the word?
Here I am.
Here I am.

Can you say the word today?
Can you spell the word today?
I can try.
I can try.

Name_____

Sight Words List/Reading Inventory

 Each week have each student read a column of sight words. Make a check mark next to each word the student skips, mispronounces, or needs your assistance with. Record these words in the student's Individual Word Profile (page 63) to indicate which words need review. Place this inventory in each student's portfolio.

	about		even		knew		play		time
	after		ever		know		please		to
	again		every		last		put		today
	all		family		light		read		too
	along		first		like		right		took
	also		for		little		round		tried
	always		found		long		said		two
	am		friend		look		saw		under
	an		from		made		school		until
	another		girl		make		sea		up
	any		go		many		see		us
	are		going		me		should		use
	around		good		might		some		very
	as		had		more		something		want
	asked		half		move		sometimes		was
	at		has		my		sure		watch
	be		have		never		take		we
	because		he		new		talk		went
	been		head		not		than		were
	before		heard		now		that		what
	began		her		of		the		when
	better		here		off		their		where
	but		his		on		them		which
	by		how		once		then		while
	can		I		one		there		who
	children		if		open		these		will
	come		I'm		or		they		with
	could		into		other		thing		words
	day		it		our		think		year
	did		its		out		this		you
	down		it's		over		thought		your
	each		just		people		through		you're

Weekly Planner

Each week photocopy this sheet and keep it in your lesson plan book. Choose new words each week. Write the activity you will to do for each day.

Sight Weekly Plan Words

Words for the Week:

Monday	
Tuesday	
Wednesday	
Thursday	
Friday	

Success with Sight Words © 1999 Creative Teaching Press

Learning Styles Inventory

☞ Photocopy this sheet for each student. Complete the inventory based on your observations, and place it in the student's portfolio.

	Yes	No
Kinesthetic Learner		
Prefers to learn by doing		
Likes to be in motion		
Uses hands		
Memorizes by doing		
Visual Learner		
Prefers to watch first, then do		
Stays focused on the task		
Notices details		
Enjoys reading		
Memorizes by seeing		
Auditory Learner		
Prefers to have instructions given verbally		
Enjoys listening to books		
Likes to be read to		
Memorizes by hearing		

Observations	Comments	Learning Style

Success with Sight Words © 1999 Creative Teaching Press

Class Learning Styles

 Record each student's learning style. Use this information to help you plan and organize your groups.

Student Name	Kinesthetic	Visual	Auditory	Comments

Success with Sight Words © 1999 Creative Teaching Press

Word Bank

How about a Try

Try 1

Try 2

Try 3

Name_____

Sight Words Record Sheet

☞ Record new sight words for each student. Note whether each word has been introduced, reviewed, or mastered. Place the completed sheet in the student's portfolio.

Sight Word	Introduced	Reviewed	Mastered

Success with Sight Words © 1999 Creative Teaching Press

Individual Word Profile

☞ Use this sheet to record each student's progress. Place this sheet in the student's portfolio.

Date	Troublesome Words	Teaching Strategies	Comments

Name_____

Writing Assessment

Student's Spelling	Correct Spelling	I Need to Remember to:

Comments

Success with Sight Words © 1999 Creative Teaching Press

Quilt Square

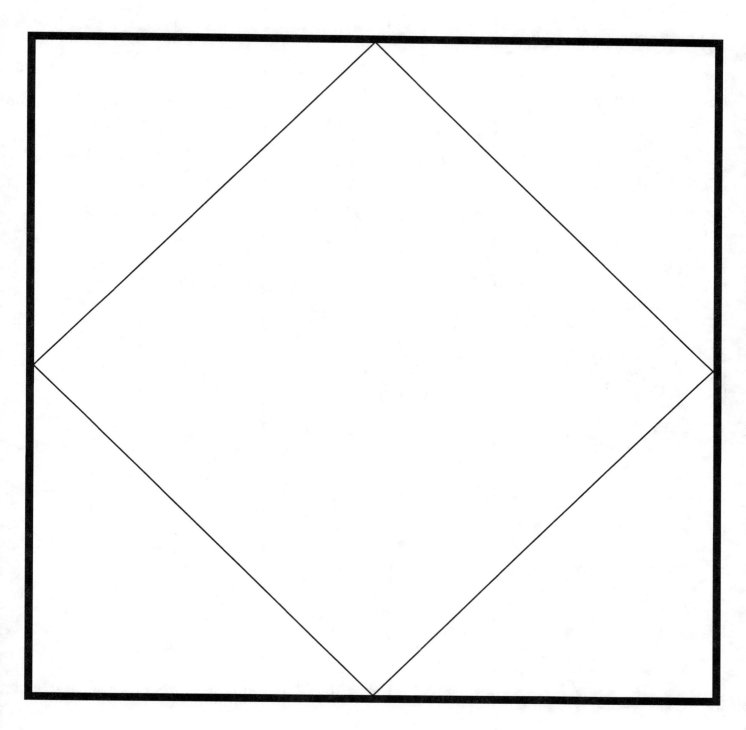

Alphabet Cards

a	b	c
d	e	f
g	h	i

Alphabet Cards

j	k	l
m	n	o
p	q	r

Success with Sight Words © 1999 Creative Teaching Press

Alphabet Cards

S	t	U
V	W	X
y	Z	

Success with Sight Words © 1999 Creative Teaching Press

Telephone

Mobile

"Sun"sational
Sight Words

Suns

Creepy Crawlers

Symbols

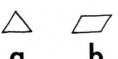 

a	b	c	d	e	f	g	h	i

j	k	l	m	n	o	p	q	r

s	t	u	v	w	x	y	z

Word Search

Success with Sight Words © 1999 Creative Teaching Press

Postcard

Word Makers

Success with Sight Words © 1999 Creative Teaching Press

Eat My Words

Word	Build the Word	Write the Word

Bingo

Graph It

Name _____

Word	1	2	3	4	5	6	7	8	9	10	11	12	13	14	15	16	17	18	19	20

Success with Sight Words © 1999 Creative Teaching Press

Stop Sign